I0659777

HENNESSY & MEMORIES: SPEECH THERAPY VOL I
LaVar Ramon Guy

HENNESSY & MEMORIES: SPEECH THERAPY VOL I
ISBN (Trade pbk.)
978-1-7330502-6-5
Layout and Design: Chris Massenburg
Cover Art: JRC3 Designs

HPJ's Writeeasy Publishing
Durham, NC

"I poured my heart out in a wine glass and offered her a drink She declined... Said she was already drunk from my past deceptions and broken promises"

Table of Contents

BLACK GIRL JUICE

Intoxicated by your smell

Hypnotized by your eyes

I fiend for your kiss,

while your thighs make me high...

I try to kick the habit

Can't do it

I'm just at an addict

Addicted and afflicted, with desires to get higher

I need to concentrate

Change my mental state

So I can demonstrate

This need to rehabilitate

But withdrawal becomes hard

I'm going thru the shakes

Can't wait to participate

In my favourite pastime

You're fine and like wine grow better with time

I find myself dreaming of you at night

As well as the middle of the day

I have to find a way to fight this addiction

Open my third eye to see a world with the same affliction

They hung up on you like they necks was in the noose

Another who fell victim to the Black Girl Juice

Black Girl Juice

Sweeter than the natural nectar flowers produce

The same sweet smelling, soothing scent

That when inhaled will seduce

The most righteous brother

No other can possess it

You are truly heaven sent

It's evident

I have no choice but to represent and compliment

Your Black Girl Juice

Black Girl Juice

In my youth, I strayed far from the truth

I even tried to reproduce the juice

With the ancestors of the same molesters

that tainted our roots

Realized why we so diverse in the colors we disperse

Caramel sundae, chocolate deluxe, butter pecan and even mocha

latte

That's why they tan to be like you...

and fuck your man just to spite you

It's aight Boo

The juice is a tool she can never use

I Refuse to compromise

Our pain and struggle are sometimes

blessings in disguise

Realize that we have to stay together

Why we gotta pray together

Before we lay together

We need to build together

We used to pick the fields together

In the hot sunny weather

While the leather whip attacked my back

Crack, smack... crack, smack

The overseers in the back

of the slave quarters raping our daughters

Diluting the potency of her Black Girl Juice

So she has to reproduce

and her baby gotta reproduce

So the juice gets a little more potent

It's important that I get my point across

They say my generation is lost

Every day I pay the cost

For being enlightened, I frighten

that man cause he can't comprehend

or understand that I'm the original man

and

from the original woman I was born

Born from the smile of Lena Horne

and the voice of Sarah Vaughan

My word is born

Strong like Harriet Tubman

Priceless like Isis who breathes life into millions just like us

It ain't no justice

It's just us

and without you

There could never be a me

They misrepresent you, Love

When they show you on TV

The media sees you as prostitutes and dope fiends

You're a Queen

and in your genes there's more than DNA

There lies the very reason

there is a "so called" civilization today

I just wanted to take the time out to say

I love y'all for all you represent

That's nothing but the truth

I'd die a million times

To live once with you and your

Black Girl Juice.

GOD-IS

She's a Goddess

A reflection of what God IS

She's flawless

Couldn't have been made from my rib

when she makes men

Awakens them to the God within

She bends but to break is forbidden

Your strength...

Immeasurable

You are truly a treasure, you

Goddess

Reflecting what God IS

You're flawless

To be honest

I'm honored to stand with you through hardships

Celebrate your triumphs

Make your problems cease to exist,

'Cause I exist to guard you

It's hard to imagine

but your scars are beauty marks

You are art and I applaud you

At times it may seem that we disregard you

You work twice as hard at the same job

But make less than he do

How is that equal

It's disgraceful

6

But you make dealing with the 'D' evils

seem beautiful

Even if you paint a smile on your face

it never seems to bother you

You, Goddess, you

Reflecting what God IS, through being flawless

I can't fathom

Being apart from you

I'm a part of you

I know it's hard for you

but remember

Goddess

God is ...Invincible

DADDY (missing you)

I began mourning that morning

Around a quarter to 5 {4:45}

Got the call from my brother,

told me that I needed to come home

Daddy had died

Down on my luck and on my last buck

Western Union don't open 'til nine

While I waited

I cried, the entire time

I ran out of tears, my eyes never been so dry

Throat filled with words left unspoken

Nose congested with memories of your unapologetic scent,

of cognac, weed, cigarettes and adolescent innocence

You were free

Sucking snot,

my ears popped with memories of melodies you would sing off key

You were everything to me

Everything I wanted to be

You were free

Never confined by what others seen

You defined individuality

You designed me and I accepted my destiny

Graciously

Your son, the youngest one

Ironically

everything you said you wanted to be

But I was merely your reflection

with my mother's tenacity

My dreams were too big for

our small city

You told me to flee quickly and never look back

Told me the trap was just that...

A trap

As a matter of fact

thinking back you were right,

I should've never questioned that

Found out you was smoking crack

I had to chase you off the block

Then get back on mine

You see

We were both victims of the grind

Your addiction was different than mine

You were chasing freedom

Me, I was chasing dollar signs

You found salvation

when they laid you in the ground

I'm still wondering when I'll find mine

Will it happen before losing my mind

Think I already have sometimes

That's why I pen these lines

GABBY

Damn I miss my Daddy

Miss my Daughter more

My Daddy made Me

But I made Her

It's crazy

Cause I couldn't save Her

begged The Lord, to "take me"

and that's when her

heart stopped beating

I cried the whole weekend

Needed to hear more than preaching

Grew tired of reaching

Never getting close enough to grab hold

The air from the top floor of the hospital was so cold

About to take my own life

like I ain't have no Soul

Heard my Daddy say "I got Her"

And... You

Got so much to live fo'

Take care of ya kinfolk

Gave you broad shoulders

So, you can carry that load

This is just a speed bump in the road

that You have to get over

to get where u need to go

I know this pain feels

insurmountable

and I'm no longer there to council you

But they all count on you

Maintain, until I can introduce you two

I needed her with me cause I couldn't have you

My son, you have so much more to do

Your daughters smile like your mama do

Your son acts like you used to

Just give them everything I gave you

Give them all of you

A Mother's Day Gift

She sleeps

Exhausted from a long work week

Pain filled cheeks

She weeps

In private

too strong to let us see

Inspired by our mere existence

Makes us feel gifted

with endless possibilities

I've paid her back with mediocrity

So this is my apology

I will make you proud Mama

I will live out my dreams

Cause I seen

too many dreams

deferred

I even watched as she sacrificed hers

For that I am grateful

You're an example of loyalty

At times a bit hateful

I understand

We were a handful but you never gave up

And for that

I am truly thankful

You nurtured my curiosities

Nursed my many injuries

A friend to so many,

I feel sorry for any enemies

Being cussed out by Nita

is one of the worst experiences,

I guarantee

I love you Mama

unconditionally

I know I've disappointed you

but I'll make you proud one day

You will see

You did the very best you could

and if you should

ever wonder if you are a great mother

Just know

I wouldn't change a minute of my life

if I could...

Motherless Child

Sometimes I feel....

Like a motherless child...

But I'm grown

and she's gone

She was all I had left

and I ain't never felt

so alone

See all my life I've been a "Mama's Boy"

Did everything I could just to bring her joy

Most times I came up short

But she loved me anyway

She was My support,

My teacher, My guide, My judge...

She was my God in human form

Been trying my whole life to be as good as she thought I was

I'm finding it hard not to hold a grudge

Why my mama have to go when all she did was show love

Maybe alone I will discover what I'm truly capable of

I no longer fear failure

Won't have to hear her cuss

But when I fall

Who will be there to pick me up

Who will be there when I need a hug

Seems it ain't no love

for a Mama's boy

Now that my Mama's gone

14

No one can fill that void

But I won't give up

'Cause one thing's for sure

She's watching to see the MAN

her baby boy becomes.

Mama (unfinished)

Used to wish that she'd mind her business

Now I'm missing her wisdom

Wondered why she always talked so loud

Now I'd silence the world to hear her voice

vibrate off my eardrums

She was love

I ain't appreciate her enough

She was tough

Her strength protected us

Everybody says "stay strong"

But I never had to be

I often see

what seems to be

The brightest star in the galaxy

and know its Nit

She was a friend to every soul she'd meet

and she was everything to me...

NC CURE

No Chances, No Choices, No Coincidence

Nigga Commit Nightly Crimes

Nigga Crowd, Nickel Crack, Nines Claps

Never-mind Consequences

Now Courts Name Cases

Narrow Clarity New Jack City

Nino Calamity

Niggas Can Never Conceive, Not Cooperating

Not Contemplating, No Cop Needs Coons

Not Cooperating

Newport Cigarettes, Nerves Calm

Now Cats, Naively Confess

Narrate Cassettes, Negate Conglomerates

Negro Cartels Need Control

Nobody Cares

New Cars, Nice Chains, Nab Chicks

Now Children Need Constant Natal Care

Nobody Cares

Narcotic Consumer, Nonchalantly, Nail Coffins

No Conscience, Now Coke, New Cotton

Need Change, Needed Christ. Never Came.

FUCK A FLAG (Kaepernick'n)

I could care less about a flag

more concerned with the badge

that rests on the chest of the cops

that keep killing our ass

The Klan without the mask

Whistling sweet Dixie

Basking in memories of the past

They chant "Make a America Great, Again"

and I can't help but laugh

My Granddaddy's Jim Crow stories

painted a different picture

Told me about my great uncle

and how the Klan tried lynch him

after he whooped one of them bad

I ain't anti-America, just can't

pledge allegiance to the flag

of the divided race in America

and to the segregated public

who don't understand

we can never be one nation

under their God

When we're denied liberty

Ain't no justice,

it's just us

and y'all.

CITY TRENDS

I got a lotta love for my city

Even though

it ain't a lot of love *in* my city

Violence is a part of history

From the public hangings in past centuries

to street fights in the 70s

We lost a lot of daddies in the 80s

to that cocaine

In the 90s we lost their sons to the crack game

Now we are losing their sons because they gang bang

It's a damn shame

3 generations dead or in chains

Still, we maintain

Until the next name

kicks off another R.I.P campaign

To the mothers of the slain

I hope time can ease your pain

To my city

I love you but maybe you're the blame

We were raised

to do the RIGHT thing

But LEFT to figure out what that means

It's Hard to dream

living in a nightmare

Hard to do well

on welfare

Hard to heal

with no health care

The HATE is so REAL, but the LOVE is so FAKE here

Only so much you can take

it's damn near impossible to escape here

Move away physically, but mentally you still here

To put it simply

When you're raised to have no fear

When things get scary

it's hard to see clear

Suppressed emotions surface

during confrontation

So, it seems fair

to hear gunshots

ring by your ear

The Post reports the story

but

you were right there

It could've been you

but you survived

Still feels like your times near

Death has become too common here

Carrying a weapon is a necessity

and that bothers me because

I got a lotta love for my city

even though it ain't a lotta of love *in* my city

The pain and the pity

The memories of friends that turned enemies

The bad energy

There's no pretending

See,

these streets have a tendency

to make you prove yourself regularly

I just wish we saw the beauty

in community

Wish we could communicate, speak unity

Give the youth something new to see

Visions of positivity

A sight

not afforded to you and me

I gotta a lotta love for my CITY!!

Even though

it ain't a lotta love *in* my city

Violence is a part of history

From the public hangings in past centuries

to street fights in the 70s

Lost a lot of daddies in the 80s

to that cocaine

In the 90s we lost their sons to the crack game

Now we are losing their sons because they gang bang

It's a damn shame

3 generations

dead or in chains

Still we maintain

But, we must change.

Black Poltergeist

My hometown is haunted

by dead slaves

whose hollers

have long been forgotten

Open graves

Confederate monuments

Civil War re-enactments

The fact is

Cotton is the fabric of our lives

The mills employed our parents

but they shutdown

Republicans made it cheaper for corporations

to pay for labor across the border

You know, the same one they trying

to put a wall around now

Middle class family was

just trying to get by

Around the same time

folks started getting high

Trying to silence their kids cries

When working men can't find jobs

they turn to crime

So the youth got very wise

Found ways to capitalize

Turned heartless

Hard to sympathize

Watching grown men

sell they soul for a hit

This so called grind

took over the minds of a people

who were once sold on the block

Just like these nicks and dimes

They made us property

but never told us our worth

They promised equality

but all they gave us was church

They said we could escape poverty

with enough hard work

Projects or the plantation

I wonder which one's worse

Ain't that much difference really

Seems we're cursed from birth

Ain't picking cotton no more

but still harvesting hurt

Hands still covered in dirt

Still asking Massa for the master plan

Overseer, Officer...

Ku Klux Klan

We shooting each other down

acting just like them

Thought if we made enough money

we could buy our freedom

or at least let us live like them

Became Intoxicated

with trying to make it

Get incarcerated,

once free men

now we just slaves again

Penitentiary or the plantation

Let that sink in

They don't use chains no more

They just fencing us in

Prison system or gentrification

Generation after generation

These youngsters feel so boxed in

that they're ready to explode

Been on prescription medication

since he was 5 years old

He has ADHD is what his Mama was told

He doesn't pay attention

He's so hard to control

Teachers are not psychologist

but she playing the role

So by 17 he's addicted

to substances unknown

He start popping pills/drinking lean

so he can get in his zone

Don't know

if he's coming or going

All he knows is that he needs coins

but ain't ready for change

I tried to tell him to maintain

He never listened

In the club popping

bottles of champagne

Then the shots came

Blood stained his Jesus chain

Tore up his young frame

from close range

Still see it plain

Still feel his pain

Still hear them scream his name

But all was silent when the cops came

Just another forgotten holler of another dead slave

26

ROLE MODELS

Positive paper seems impossible

And positive role models mythological

Two black men had stores in my hood,

there were a few barbers,

and one black dentist, but they was all tenants

Buildings rented from redneck crackers

who never patronized they business

So I ask forgiveness

for what you had to witness

when we started to distribute

crack cocaine a few feet from your entrance

I'm sorry we didn't wanna listen

to how you rode buses from Montgomery to Memphis

singing spirituals while you waited on Jesus

See your visions of freedom, ain't what we seeing

Our mothers work in factories, our fathers out here feenin'

We stop dreaming, ain't no more singing

"We shall overcome"

We grabbing guns fighting for our freedom

End up killing each other for no damn reason

Cooped up in the projects season after season

Products of neglect, Generation X

You wanted equality, but became slaves to the check

The nerve of you to judge

Entrepreneurial spirit

We trying to get it

You told us go to college

but we skipped it

We got dope and flipped it

Cried out for help

Y'all didn't hear it

or you dismissed it

Called us misfits

Told us we were unfit

to follow your blueprint

We just think it's nonsense

to walk in your footsteps

Been marching since Martin

Ain't got shit accomplished yet

Officials elect officers to serve and protect

But all these overseers serve us is death

and protect the interest

of those who invest

Capitalism at its best

They got they foot on my neck

I'm yelling I can't breathe

Selling cigarettes or CDs could lead

to 6 shots to the chest

Can't walk to the store for skittles or cigarillos,

Can't reach for ID when I'm in the car

with my daughter and wifey

or my body might get riddled with shots

They say it's 6 million ways to die

and one is interaction with cops

Went from patty rollers asking for freedom papers

To these racists asking for paper at traffic stops

The illusion of freedom got people

believing that being a victim is our fault

We were brought here for labor

They never thought

we'd have a seat at the table

We was taught

to work hard as long as we able

And that a white man died on the cross

to send us an angel

Who promised salvation

through a series of fables

It ain't hard to tell

They want us looking forward to heaven

so we can keep ignoring this hell

BROKEN

To all the souls

Broken…but not yet finished

The ones who replay images

of memories so vivid

The pain still feels

as real

as when you were first injured

Wish you could see the bigger picture

The past can never change

But to truly see the future

you gotta keep living

Can't give in

Can't keep asking for permission

to protect your own existence

You owe yourself forgiveness

for innocence lost while

daydreaming during nightmares

Waking up to cold stares

from a demon in an angel's disguise

Her eyes hold the reflection of a willing slave

As we lay,

she plays tour guide thru my darkest days

I found heaven between her thighs

It was really an early grave

I've died a thousand times

Only broken pieces remain

But I'm not finished

I've gathered what's left of me

Piece by piece, can't nobody love me,

like I love me

You must create the peace,

you so desperately seek

To all the souls

Broken

But not yet finished

The ones who

replay images

of memories so vivid

The pain still feels

as real

as when you were first injured

Wish you could see the bigger picture

'Cause I been there

My vision wasn't any clearer

Staring at the man in the mirror

asking him to change his ways

Just because they can't see your worth

Doesn't mean you must look at yourself the same.

TRUTH IS

The truth is

I spend more time with my tears

than I do with my kids

It's not fair

but it's just the way that it is

I brought it upon myself

I was conquered by fear

Once told by an angel that each blessing is watered by tears

I wait patiently for my harvest to appear

Cause I been watering that garden for years

These tears have clouded my vision

and it's

hard to see clear

My blessings already here

Even if I can't hold them near

I hope

they know

I care

I never prepared

for this season

Still no reason

to give up

I stare at their pictures

To watch them grow up

But, it's not enough

The truth is

I spend more time with my tears

than I do with my kids

And it's all my fault,

I fucked up

Learned a lesson about consequences

Karma always catches up

They say you never miss your well

until the water dry up

I just wanna be present when my daughter wakes up

When the sun rises

Watch my son rise

They're my light, in a world of darkness

But I'm just a Father

The powers that be don't give a damn about us

Pay what they say or get locked up

They made paying child support

more important, than raising our young

Miss a payment

No visit

I've strained my tear ducts

Burning sensation in my eyes

Is this the hell they speak of?

It's all unjust and corrupt

All because

I didn't wanna wait in vain

for her love

She tamed the beast in me

then gave me 2 cubs

Got pissed at me

and then she snatched them both up

I sacrificed everything to make sure she came up

Now she look down on me like I didn't do much

The truth is our kids

ain't never wanted for nothing

So fuck family court

I ain't coming the next time I'm summoned

Cause they ain't trying to hear me at the hearing

I'm just a father In their eyes

My opinion means nothing

I'm noncustodial

In other words,

pay what you owe

But when it comes to decisions

about my children

I have no say-so

I could petition the court

but I could lose

and she might not let me see them no more

So the truth is

I take what I can get

Still I spend more time with my tears

than I do with my kids

It's not fair

It just is what it is

So I appreciate

every second with them

I'm number one in their eyes

I'm never second to them

Trying to catch a second wind

Preparing for the battle of my life

versus this wicked system.

CHEAPER 2 KEEP HER

They say it's cheaper to keep her

But I told myself

I ain't really need her

She told me I wasn't shit

and I believed her

Eager

to prove her right

I lost sight on how to treat her

Once an overachiever

Now I act like I ain't see her

I was busy trying to feed us

I'm thankful that she freed us

I would've wasted my forever

chasing a Love, I've never seen once

I realized that I ain't mean much

I was just supplemental income

and a familiar touch

Then one holy night

My stroke was right

And WE became Gods

as we laid

A galaxy was made

And she gave birth to two stars

That's when it got hard

Cause they shined their light so bright

and she dimmed hers

They showed me unconditional love

They filled a void

An emptiness

that I could no longer ignore

The universe never gives

more than one can endure

I'm not sure cause losing her

hurt me to the core

A feeling I've never really felt before

They say it's cheaper to keep her

But I could no longer afford

to give my peace up

So I destroyed pieces

of her

After I spent several seasons saving her

Her knight in shining armor

Guess I liked her better when she was healing

That feeling

of being needed

I need it

Back then we were in agreement

That she was my greatest achievement

The woman of my dreams meant

more to me than my own sanity

I mean it's egregious

To think that I put her on a pedestal

Just for her to look down on me

To think that I was willing to go to war for her

but she wouldn't fight a round for me

She could've stuck around for me

But the minute she could no longer benefit

from our partnership

I got dismissed and she vanished, quick

Then turned around and made me the author of her narrative

Responsible for failed marriage

It's not hard to imagine

You didn't need me anymore

But before you threw me away

I decided to ruin the rest of your days

I felt betrayed

by the woman I helped create

The old you would've never been this brave

To say the things you say,

and the way you behave

The old you would be ashamed

What happened to my teammate

I made mistakes but these games you play

make me look at you strange

Why is my children's mother

entertaining these mother fuckin lames

Cause I destroyed you?

Or is it for financial gain?

Either way

Guess I'll bear the blame....

I only did it 'cause you destroyed me

And I ain't wanna be broken alone

You gave up on me

I never got a chance to atone

Nor right my wrongs

So now I roam

and write my wrongs

in these here poems

Trying to find my heart a home

My self-worth was once contingent

upon your approval

Had to check myself

Now I accept myself

on my own

I guess I've grown

I'm so far gone

I've lost interest

In trying to get credit

to still end up alone {a loan}

'Cause they say it's cheaper to keep her

But what's the price of freedom

when ya Queen denounces her throne.

ENOUGH

I say

she don't love me enough

But she loved me as much

as she could

Could've used

my help

My selfish ways

got In the way

Paid back in days

Alone with memories

She was a friend to me

when I needed one

so desperately

Turned enemy

She only wanted the best for me

but I was too focused on the rest of me

The pain, the fear, the anxiety

taking the very breath I breathe

I wanted her to invest in me

But I ain't have no equity

It was imperative that I became

a better me

She recognized my light

But I was blinded by insecurity

I ain't love myself enough

But I loved myself as much

as I could

Should've used

her help

But my selfish

ways

got in the way

I still thought she would save me

She gave up and I can't blame her

Really

LOVE DON'T LIVE HERE

She used to have me feeling great

King Kong on the Empire State

Holding her in my arm as I swat

the dangers of the world away

Just me and my Bae

But as of late

I'm alone on the Empire State

On roller skates

My entire fate

Depends on whether or not she holds me down

Feels like I'm cheating somehow

Cause the beauty I used to hold

Ain't this beast I see now

See in this house there's no sound

Like when the kids are asleep

Or there is no one around

When it's just us

Instead of fuss

We say nothing at all

Love don't live here no more

And I just found out

Apparently, love been leaving for a while

Slowly packing away smiles every time we wild out

We fussing then fucking

touching then cussing

But never discussing our vows

We fell in love

but couldn't stand in it

We just kept falling down

When I got down

on one knee

I offered my eternity

But she forever pissed at me now

Cause her decision was bout business

My head stayed in the clouds

Cause I thought you and I (u n i)

Started a UNIon

Began the UNIverse

I'm the sun

You the earth

But you're rude

and I'm worse

I love you

You wanna purse

I know your worth

Galaxies

But I gotta make it thru earth first

And it's gone take hard work

But I can do it Baby

I just may need your help

Extended my arm; open palm

Just take one step

She left

Love don't live here no more

I'm by myself....

Ironically

I love the company

I got used to

When she let the comforter

Comfort her

And slept so comfortably

in a bed there was no room for me

Living room walls felt like a tomb to me

Love songs sound out of tune to me

But I refuse to let you ruin me

What the fuck happened to you and me??

We had a love I thought was indestructible

We used to get high and watch the Huxtables

Eat up the kids lunchables

I thought I was enough for you

Maybe I was too much for you

Showed you a few

things that you never really seen

Your Momma left your Daddy

Your Uncle left your Auntie

Your Grandma stayed

But y'all begged her to leave

Your desolate disease

Started effectively infecting me

Causing asphyxiation

I can't breathe

I need a quarantine

What gives you the credentials

to critique me or even try and define

what a man should be

I'm King .... Kong

Atop the Empire State

Feeling Great

My entire fate

Depends on whether or not I hold me down

It's about me now

Love don't live here no more

I'm glad I finally found out!

HURT YOU, HURT ME

I hurt you

You hurt me

Two wrongs don't make no right

I love you

You loved me

but two loves couldn't make no life

We fought

long and hard

Went to war over a facade

Forever at odds over a mirage

These are the cards

we were dealt

Never mind how we felt

all those late nights, laughing

staring at the stars

Things seem so simple

But they rarely are

We made it hard

Both wanted to be in charge

Ignored our scars

Now I sit alone at the bar

Hoping to find my heart

in the bottom of a glass

Guess it's worth a shot

Maybe not

Gotta stop

living in the past

Faded pictures in a broken glass

If life is what we make it

Why we couldn't make it

...last?

How could we remain one?

Traveling different paths

All the laughs

that we shared

couldn't prepare

me for the tears

I swear

life is so unfair

I wish you were right here

I stare

at the other side of the bed

but you're not there

I toss and turn

wallowing in despair

Trying to repair

what's left of my heart

but I don't know where to start

So, I roll up my thoughts

and

ART AT ODDS

We used to make art

Now we at odds

We spar like we boxing

So I grabbed an old shoebox

A notebook and two pens

I said let's write down all our grievances

Throw the pages in the box and leave them shits

Dig a hole and bury all of that pain

Under the tree where we once carved our names

We fell like leaves in Fall

We produced amazing fruit

for two Springs

I thought we died that Winter

Then I remembered that seasons change

For whatever reason we both came

at the same time the first time

And we ain't been the same

since

We spent season after season watching the leaves

leave

Instead of seizing opportunities to

enjoy our growth

I realize that words hurt

When we spell, we cast spells

I projected pain and

didn't appreciate your worth

I try to express myself

But can't find the words that work

You say words ain't enough

Waitaminute

Didn't u just say my words fucked you up

Then why can't these words pick you up?

I'm stuck

Somewhere in between if it's meant to be

it'll be

and just giving the fuck up

Sorry didn't mean to curse you

No con in this verse

Can we converse truth?

Engage in an exchange of positivity

Just me and my muse.

Hennessy and Memories

Together our energies don't blend

I'm repenting but you seeking revenge

It's a fucked up situation

Cause we used to be friends

That wasn't enough for me

I wanted you to have my kids

And you did

Selfishly

I poured my all into them

Took you for granted

I ain't plan it

Understand, It

was how I tried to prove my worth

to you

Show my gratitude for your sacrifice

But I guess I ain't do it right

So each night I write

Trying to figure out life

How we got to this point

and what's the point

Losing my voice

Arguing with ears that only hear

Memories

I sip Hennessy

Trying to drown out the imagery

Cause loving you is fucking up my energy

seriously.

I LOST (EYE LOST)

I got lost in her eyes

Been trying to find

my way back ever since

Spent

too much time chasing the wind

All I had to do was be still

To know that it's real

To feel doesn't require a clinch

To heal doesn't require revenge

You can pretend

To mend

torn relationships

Piecing together sections of bliss

with kisses and memories of karma sutra positions

Common sutures, conceal the truest intentions

Not to mention

you miss your friend

Your day ends

Covered in this quilted highlight reel

that is not real

Knowing in the morning reality gon' set in

and You're alone again

Lost in eyes that don't see you the same

as they did back then

Going insane trying to escape them

Caught wind

That she had a special friend

So what was oh so special then

You have given away without getting at me

That's your fault,

how many times you forgiven me?

How was I to know that you was plain sick of me?

I know the way a nigga living was whack

but you don't get a nigga back like that!

Shit I'm a man with pride, you don't do shit like that

You don't just pick up and leave and leave me sick like that

You don't throw away what we had, just like that

I was just out chasing wind, I was gon' get right back

They say you can't turn a bad girl good

But once a good girl's gon bad, she's gone forever..

I'll mourn forever

Shit I gotta live with the fact I did you wrong forever...

But that ain't living

And I ain't Jigga

I won't say never

Every ending is a new beginning

Loving you is my new religion

Cause I spent so much time lost in your eyes

I finally see your perception

View your progression

Baptized in your tears

Crucified in your iris

Realized you're Isis

Responsible for my resurrection

You're priceless

and loved me through all my transgressions

We've transitioned

to God and Goddess

From Mr. & Mrs.

TV GUIDE

I'm not telling you to get over the past

Just don't make me stay there with you

I got issues

Need a resolution

Need a revolution

This constant confusion

Too time consuming

Pursuing the very thing that got you ruined

Trying to piece together the artifacts

like you an archaeologist

But you don't know what the fuck you're doing

It's

never happening

like a **Cosby** show reunion

You in a **Different World** girl

Family Matters

That's just the **Facts of Life**

Had

Good Times with **My Wife and Kids**

But **What's Happening Now**

is just a *Rerun*

of **The Game** we played when we were

Living Single but

those **Days of Our Lives** are over

You were a **Teenage Mom**

Made you the **Boss** early

I was a **Jackass** on the **Corner** unworthy

I wanted **Power**

but ended up the **Biggest Loser**

That fate left me **Scared Straight**

And by this time, you were screaming

Gimmie a Break

Under my breath

I asked you where u wanted it

Cause I wanna **MASH** your face in

Visions of **Knots Landing**

I wanna pluck your forehead

You make me so **Mad TV** is no longer **Entertainment Tonight**

We going thru **Growing Pains**

I'm growing up

We growing apart

I **Wonder Years** ago

If I would've just let go

of my ego

Made **Home Improvement**

Went to **Couples Therapy**

Our **Modern Family**

wouldn't Be in **Jeopardy**

I mean who knows

We could've been more

than just

Married with Children

But **Life Goes On**

And a *Family Feud*

in *Divorce Court*

ain't gonna prove whose right or wrong

Just *Law and Order* so the real issue still unresolved

Unsolved Mystery

You can't love me and your misery

I mean *Threes Company*

But I feel *Lost* when you right in front of me

I'm a *Survivor*

but the *Real World* Is a *Challenge*

Alone

I'm off balance

Trying the *Dating Game* but it's full of *Cheaters*

Ain't find no *Real Housewives*

Just misguided *Divas*

Plenty of *Sex in City*

but I can't get Carrie'd away

So rather than get caught up in *Scandal*

I chill and burn reefer

Being Mary Jane is my new boo thang

I'm high above your Revenge plot

You *Wild'n Out* with *Hollywood Squares*

But if you *Press your Luck* long enough

You gone be with them *Single Ladies*

until you a *Golden Girl*

In the *Heat of the Night*

I was an *Undercover Boss*

Giving you **Different Strokes**

Making your toes curl

We had a **Real Chance at LOVE**

but the real died

Spent the **First 48** hours

trying to figure out this **Murder She Wrote**

Realized I was living on **Fantasy Island**

and no matter how hard I tried

This love couldn't **Blossom** {Wooooa}

Hindsight **20/20**

No more edits our show over

And

I'm still looking for the credit

CLUMSY

You put your heart in my hands

knowing I'm clumsy

How many times I had to pick myself up

You helped me put the pieces back together

Now I perfectly position my person in your peripheral

Hoping you 'll catch a view

Or at least

get a glimpse of me

But she dismisses me

Like there is nothing new to see

In fact she's

quite familiar

Still I hope she'll get past

my torn exterior

To appreciate a soul

that no longer feels inferior

I am undeserving of

ya love....

But can you look at me?

I am not your enemy

I need your energy

Consistently

I vividly remember the ending of we

Us

     You

Me

58

Them

Soul sister

My Queen

My love

My friend

My life's poem that never ends

So don't pretend

that you can't see me

when you look within

I'm clumsy

But I'm trying my best

not to fall again

I'm trying hard to shake this mood I'm in

I just want to be whole again

Holding in

Feelings

Until I lose control of them

They escape

Leaving holes within

My soul

That need filling in

I feel the emptiest

when I'm full

of discontent

These problems

Like squatters

Occupy residence

without paying rent

But if they vacate the premises

I'd be left with more holes and

back in the same predicament

See I need the pain

cause hurting feels better than feeling nothing at all

I'm trying hard to shake this mood I'm in

I just wanna be whole again

I just wanna have her to hold again

I just wanna touch her skin

Every chance I get

I remember how wet she'd get

I would lick

and suck and kiss her lips

Stiff tongue her hole while

my top lip

massaged her clit

I would not stop until she begged for it

Placed her legs upon my shoulders

then I buried dick

Trying to touch her soul with each stroke

Haven't matched that passion yet

Her waters quenched my thirst

I'm dehydrated

Trying hard to shake the mood I'm in

I just want to be whole again

She makes me whole

Her feelings

fill in holes in my soul

But leave her empty ....

I'm clumsy

SPACE INVADERS

I'm sorry

I used you as the container for my

overflow of insecurity

But since

You filled me with your history of misery

Told me

how the pain left drained and empty

I figured you had

space

until you said you needed yours

Closed doors

On conversations

Frustrated

I tried to find the right combination

But grew impatient

As I imagined unlocking the secret

of your forgotten smile

Never knew the key

was being a better me

and honestly

I'd become complacent

Feared that you had found my replacement

Instead of concentrating on changing

So I wouldn't need replacing

Busy chasing dreams

I slept on my biggest supporter

Never showed her

that she mattered

Matter of fact

The mattress outlasted

the disaster

we disguised as marriage

Artificial love

One sided hugs

Mastered

the magic of make believe

with theatrics

That would leave

Walt Disney inspired

Belle!

The Beast is tired

I was never meant to be tame

It's a shame

The way we ended up

was corny as fuck

That wasn't never really supposed be us

You lost trust

in me

Truth is I'd rather be

a memory

Since it seems my presence

don't matter so much

So when you smile randomly

when you think of me

Realize you

fulfilled your prophecy

Cause your light was only

meant to lead me

to all the places

I could never see

I could never be,

who you wanted me to be

Especially

Since what you want changes daily

Barely able to be what I need for me

I mean

I lived your dream so long

that I slept on me

Exhausted, lost my energy

Finally found my inner G

Now I vibrate on a different frequency

Thank you for releasing me

I hope you cleared the space you needed

TIME

It's only 3 hours early she says...

Like 180 minutes isn't a long time

But there are only 168 hours in a week

60 of those I spend working

5 more hours adding the commute

And since I'm only ALLOWED 48 hours with my youths....

Yes 3 hours seems like a lifetime

To you they're children

To me they're my lifeline

I need them like oxygen

And before I start to cry again

I need you to understand

that 3 hours is a long fucking time

I've obeyed every guideline and paid every dime

So, I need all my time

Your tactics are not sublime

You like playing with my mind

I see the game in your eyes as you reply,

"u know where we stay come by anytime"

Like when I pick them up

You beg for me to come inside

Like when we fucked I picked you up

and you begged for me to cum inside

I did

Now I have to ask to come inside

to see what's half mine

My kids

See u ain't a single mother

You a single woman

with kids

For them

I'm still with you Stride for stride

But for us I'm done

I have no more time

I should read you this shit

when you arrive

But I won't

U probably wouldn't have the time....

The time is 4:45am and I can't sleep

I scroll the pictures saved in my phone

Alone

Tears and memories the only company I keep

Weak

Hard to make it through the week

Their smiles are all I need

All I want

All I see

Nothing else really matters to me

My history of not knowing me

is the main factor that leads

to my current situation

so I use poetry as therapy

Words battle feelings of inadequacy

I'm broken, shattered the possibility

of my happy ever after

Thoughts of their laughter

plays in my head like a broken record

as I navigate through this unnatural disaster

Their images are plastered

on the back of my eyelids

so closing my eyes doesn't matter

Insomnia has become my master

Work as much as I can all week,

counting hours like sheep

Hoping it makes Friday come faster

I no longer have sense of time

But they give me peace of mind

cause just the thought of looking

in their eyes justifies my grind

My life is no longer mine

My heart occupied

I die a little inside every time we say goodbye

In the meantime, I just get by

www.ingramcontent.com/pod-product-compliance
Lightning Source LLC
Chambersburg PA
CBHW070824260626
47161CB00006B/2394